OVERCOMING A LIFE DESTROYED

THE DEVASTATING IMPACT OF MENTAL ILLNESS: HOW IT TOOK MY SON'S LIFE AND ALMOST MINE

JILL D'ARPINO

authorHOUSE

AuthorHouse™
1663 Liberty Drive
Bloomington, IN 47403
www.authorhouse.com
Phone: 1 (800) 839-8640

Published by AuthorHouse 06/15/2020

ISBN: 978-1-7283-5131-5 (sc)
ISBN: 978-1-7283-5130-8 (e)

Library of Congress Control Number: 2020904969

Cover by Jill D'Arpino
Created by Sergey Velikoluzhskiy

Print information available on the last page.

Acknowledgments

I want first to thank my daughter Nicole and my partner Joe for being my life savers and Joe my rock. For all the support you have given me through many dark days that weren't easy and many days that still aren't. Thank you for staying by my side.

Thank you, Joe, for helping me with my book and for great ideas with the content and verbiage when I was stuck.

I want to thank my therapist Amy, who is an inspiration to me and keeps pushing me to move forward.

Lastly, thank you to my close friends and to all the friends that I have never met on social media, for your kind words of encouragement, love and support.

This book is dedicated to my son, Michael

so many, if's, could have's, should have's

such a hole that he left

how I treasure the littlest things

my last Mother's Day card

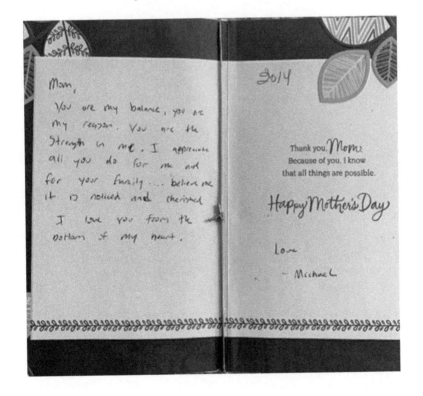

Foreword

SUICIDE

The word suicide caught your attention, didn't it? The truth is suicide catches everyone's attention. It's the actions that lead up to suicide that go unnoticed.

This book deals with the lessons I've learned about the warning signs of mental illness and the potentially devastating effects I and countless others have experienced. My dominant intention in sharing my story is to help those who are experiencing depression in their lives. To help those who have experienced the loss of a loved one or a friend by suicide. And to help anyone whose friend or loved one is showing signs of depression. My story includes steps individuals can take to begin their journey of repair as well as small things they can do to help others.

This book is about much more than a suicide survivor's loss. It's not just about my son dying, but about how I survived the tsunami that hit me when my son took his life.

As traumatic events unfolded in my life, I experienced passive suicidal ideation, post-traumatic stress disorder (PTSD), and Major depressive disorder (MDD). After my son's suicide, six months later, my then-husband left the marriage by text. I had a full hip replacement and two hospitalizations within four months, all of this happened in the first nine months of Mike's suicide. I was emotionally and mentally bankrupt. These experiences have opened my eyes to what depression is and can do to a person (including me). While the depths of despair may vary person to person, the hell, loneliness, and ultimate giving up on life need to be understood and talked about to encourage those who so desperately need help to reach out. I write at length about this in the last chapter.

Mental illness and suicide are finally beginning to receive the attention it deserves. There is still so much more work to be done. The stigma, embarrassment, and isolation attached to mental illness keep many people silent, therefore not receiving the care they need. Suicide has risen by 40% and is a crisis! Suicide *is a silent killer.* Untreated depression is the number one cause of suicide (Suicide.org).

If you are a suicide loss survivor or suffer from depression or PTSD, this is likely to be the most traumatic event of your life. Surviving may seem like the hardest thing you've ever done. It has been for me.

I wrote this book for those of you who see a reflection of yourself, close friends, or relatives in my story and can use it as a guide. I had bought just about every book available on suicide loss survivors, loss of a child, depression, etc. Nothing resonated with me or with everything I was going through and feeling; I didn't know where to start with it all. No one understood what had just happened or could help me on that fateful day. My life was shattered and destroyed. My son had never mentioned or tried to commit suicide before. He was a Robin Williams, always making people laugh. I hope my story can help you through the darkness and in finding your way to the other side.

My experiences and observations are condensed into this one book. I will talk about surviving my son's suicide, as well as mental illness, PTSD, and passive and active suicidal ideation—which I've suffered with since my son's suicide—and what I've done to stay alive. The mental illness' I suffered has been a crippling disease, personally, and can be for those who have experienced it through a loved one.

My story is arranged chronologically through the first weeks, months, first full year, and beyond. I have no degrees or alphabets after my name, only real raw honesty, and experience. My intention is not to tell you what to do or how to feel. I cannot provide a clinical diagnosis or advise you to take medication. What I can say with certainty is that it will get better with support and a great deal of work on your part. One minute, one hour, one day at a time. **Suicide is never the answer.**

I spent a lot of time researching, trying to understand what my son might have been thinking and why this happened. I came across a YouTube video in 2015 and found this young man named Kevin Hines, who was one of the very few to have survived jumping off the Golden Gate Bridge. I would go back and watch it, over and over. I'm from the Bay area, so I know that bridge and have been over it many times. It is huge and ominous.

Kevin described his manic depression, psychosis, and emotional pain that was all-consuming, and so intense that he could not think of anything but ending the pain. He expressed unwavering love for his parents but admitted that in that brief moment, he could not even think of them or the pain he would inflict. One of the hardest things a surviving person can try to reconcile after the loss of a loved one. The person suffering is incapable of worrying about the effects on family, friends, other than to apologize in some cases. He went on to say that he alone knew the extent of the hopelessness and helplessness that he felt. I could see and feel his pain.

I got a chance to meet him at one of his speeches in Delaware in May of 2019. He has a great sense of humor. I gave him a big hug and told him how he'd helped me try and understand the loss of my son to suicide and what he might have been thinking, as well as the depression/PTSD I now suffer with since my son's death. I thanked him for all he does to help people that struggle. He was very humble. He was frail, and his hand shook at the end of his two-hour speech from the pain he still feels and endured when he hit the water at seventy-five miles per hour after falling twenty-five stories in four-seconds. He still suffers from his medical challenges. Since his jump in September 2000, Kevin has had fifteen psychiatric-ward stays over the last nineteen years. He continues with his medication to manage his disease. Helping yourself is a lifelong commitment.

My biggest takeaway was *why* he jumped and what he thought when he went through with it. Since I was not able to ask my son questions, I hoped he was thinking the same. When Kevin asked other survivors what they had thought after they jumped, every single one said the same thing. "The millisecond my hands left the rail, I had instant regret." "The moment I jumped to my death was the moment I wanted to live." "No one will know I didn't want to die."

Please visit https://youtu.be/WcSUs9iZv-g, to watch a short video and hear his story.

Follow me on Twitter, Instagram, Facebook, and Youtube

https://www.youtube.com/channel/UCCh5-WFzwuFPSzPE1 plsvPA?view_as=subscriber

You may contact me at jill@aftermathofsuicide.com.

Visit my website at AftermathofSuicide.com.

Chapter One

The Text

I am a silent killer. I am indiscriminate, and I can strike without warning. I not only kill but destroy the lives of those that are left behind.

I cause chaos and trauma. Those that have not come into contact with me are frightened to utter my name for fear that I will touch their lives.

They don't realize that the only way you can stop me is to talk about me.

I am Depression-I am Suicide

Raise Awareness-Stop the Stigma

The text came through at 9:02 a.m. on December 27, 2014. I looked at my phone and panicked. My son had never sent anything like that, and I'd known he'd meant it. I'd jumped off my seat and called him. I texted him over and over and pleaded, "Please, Mike, don't do this! We will help you!" Loss of hope doesn't wait. My entire family was calling and texting him.

My son's text:

"I'm going out to visit Pop, but I'm not coming home. I have struggled with depression all my life... I just can't take it anymore. I'm sorry, I'm, so, so sorry I'm so selfish in my decision today. I can't bear it anymore; I'm so sorry. Please ask God to forgive me and my actions today. I went to church before I came out here and asked myself, but I don't know... I'm so sorry; I wished I got killed in Iraq to keep you all from my selfish decision today. These last months of my life were the happiest I have ever been, thank you all for giving me such a great life. I'm sorry, please remember the funny me."

Full panic mode set in, and I began calling the cemetery, the police, anyone I could think of that could help. Our efforts would prove futile. So many thoughts went through my mind; 90% of me knew what had already happened and kept me stopped in time: numb, empty, and feeling the devastation of an irreversible loss. The remaining 10% of me believed he would be found alive. I could still remember when he would walk in the door, his beard grazing my jaw as he greeted me with a kiss on the cheek. I could see his face. I heard his voice. I could smell him.

Would I have ever thought my life would be like this? Oh, my god! How can you possibly prepare for the death of a child? The loss from dying by suicide is so very different and often more significant than any other type of damage. At times, my mind wanders to the day I had him: the labor; Aunt Julie, his godmother, and my mom there at the hospital in Lake Tahoe. Is this a nightmare? My mind fixated on the *should* haves, *ifs, whys,* and *could have.*

Everything had to be down to a T with Mike. A mild sufferer of OCD, he was fantastically organized and paid an excessive amount of attention to detail, right down to his suicide text—229 words of detail was a hell of a lot of words. It's strange to say, but at least we got one. Many survivors have no reason why and no insights or *closure,* whatever that means. I know that I will never receive *closure* from my son's death.

Mike had suffered from depression on and off since the age of six. I had no idea a six-year-old could be depressed, but what did we know about depression thirty years ago? Especially in children? He'd never worked through all of the compounded grief he had accumulated from my father's death, a prior break-up, and his chaplain's suicide. My father died unexpectedly on June 2, 2009, the same day; Mike flew back from Iraq. A long-term relationship ended in 2013. Then Mike's chaplain—who was his best friend—took his life on January 11, 2014, eleven months before my son did. Chaplain and Mike were very close, but not nearly as close as Mike had been to my father. The hits just kept on coming.

I'd felt like a bad mother greeting my son with the unexpected news that Pop had died. It had been a bittersweet day. My son was home, yet my dad had just died. I was struggling as well, at the loss of the greatest father and grandfather. My son deserved a better homecoming then that.

It affects me to this day. I am still plagued by guilt as if somehow, I could have changed the outcome of the news. I remember the sobs I heard coming from Mike when I'd told him. He'd been inconsolable and never was quite the same again. Mike was so devastated by my dad's death. He never dealt with any of his grief or the new horrors he'd experienced in the military.

I think that was the start of the major downfalls for him in 2009. Dealing with recently experienced grief right away is extremely important! Do not think you can do this on your own!

Mike had never dealt with any loss well; all it took was one more thing. His demons, depression, and loss of hope won that terrible morning.

I was living every parent's worst nightmare. We gave him a good life. We loved him. He loved us. He laughed. He made others laugh. Then WHY? The most burning question for me was why he choose to leave us. I felt his death was a rejection of his life with us. I couldn't understand why our love for him wasn't enough to keep him alive. Since then, I've come to the ultimate reconciliation that what happened had nothing to do with his love for us. It had been all about his pain and sad reality.

That morning, we all called the Veterans Memorial Cemetery, where my dad is laid to rest, Mike was probably there. They said they had received many calls for him. My whole family was calling in, frantic! I was out of town and had a grueling seven-hour drive back. I kept calling Mike's dad, Steve, to see if anyone had heard from Mike. I called my daughter as she was trying to find and use his passwords to see if he might have left some type of clue. Nothing. We thought and hoped that maybe he'd gone up to Lake Tahoe where he was born and didn't mean what he'd texted us, but needed to clear his head.

My mind went everywhere, trying to think of where else he could be, but I also didn't want to believe that he'd meant what he'd written. In the meantime, Steve, Mike's dad, was driving to the cemetery, which was a thirty to forty-five-minute ride south to Boulder City, Nevada, from Las Vegas. Mike had almost forty-five minutes to change his mind; I'd kept thinking. When Steve got to where my dad is laid to rest, he saw yellow tape all around and police cars and started crying immediately. He parked, then the policeman came up to the vehicle and spoke with him and asked if he wanted to identify the body. Steve said no. The policeman showed him a driver's license—it was Mike's. He broke down sobbing. The search was over. No more calls, looking for him, or texting. No more **hope**. Now he had to give all of us the terrible news. He told me he'd dreaded telling me the most.

I was on my way home from California and had stopped to get something to eat, even though I was not hungry. I called Mike's dad as I walked outside Denny's restaurant to hear if he had any news on Mike. It was 12:30 p.m. I knew by the sound of his voice. Quietly, he said, "He's gone."

I fell to the ground screaming, crying, "NO! NO! NO!"

In that instant, my life had changed, and I would never be the same. My son was dead at thirty years old. My Michael? "NO! NO! NO!" I kept screaming and crying.

I would soon come to learn that I would not just be mourning my son's death, but the part of *me* that died with him: the old *me,* my past *life,* a marriage that would soon be ending, and I would be moving across the country. Depression, passive and active suicidal ideation (see Chapter Four), and post-traumatic stress disorder would soon follow. Nothing had prepared me for this, no matter how strong I was. The change that was in store for me over the next several years would change the course of my life forever.

Bill, my husband, at the time, came out of Denny's when he heard me screaming. He rushed over as did other people in the parking lot, not knowing what had happened. I don't remember much except that he wanted to take me to a hospital as I was crying and speaking incoherently. I said no, and that I wanted to get home. My thoughts were that I wanted to get on the next plane. I didn't know what the best thing to do was. No matter how I looked at it, I was not going to get home much faster, whether by waiting for the next flight home or driving. Of all times to be away from my son. That was the longest and worst day of my life. I wasn't there on *that day!* To this day, when I think about that, I close my eyes and feel sick.

It was the only Christmas I had not spent with my children. Bill's mother had cancer, and I'd thought we should go there to be near her. I'd felt so much guilt knowing I was never away from my kids at

Christmas. It had been Mike's last Christmas, and I was not there. If I'd only known, I would have turned around and run to him.

Mike's last spoken words to me on the speaker at my sister's house were, "Merry Christmas Mom, I love you!" The same words in his text to me Christmas morning. The last words I would hear.

I was beside myself and losing my mind at the same time over the death of my son, and didn't know the massive amount of guilt that I would put on myself for not being there. For the possibility that maybe *if* I had been there, he would not have left that morning. The never-ending sickening feeling that I could have made a difference *if* I had been there. The *if's, should* haves, *could* haves, and *why's* that would soon follow. It would become part of my vocabulary.

The nature of suicide makes the aftermath damn near impossible to navigate compared to any other type of loss.

I called my friends and different family members, crying and crying, on autopilot. They said they could hardly understand me. Everyone was shocked. The body's way of coping with trauma is through shock. I pulled in the driveway to go into my house. My daughter, Nicole, and her boyfriend were there for Christmas week. Her dad, Steve, came over to tell her that her brother was dead. He later told me that when he'd told her, he had to hold her up as she'd nearly fainted, and her face had turned green.

Nicole, who was twenty-five at the time, told me, "When dad went out to greet you, I sobbed knowing what he was going to tell you." Her brother—my son—had shot himself in the head, in his truck where my dad is laid to rest.

Here is a poem written by Beverly Levin Copeland about her friend's son, who shot himself as my son did. I picture my son on *that* morning as I read it.

An Ending - in Memory of Isaac

The blackest possible darkness descends.
The walls come closing in.
Fear, exhilaration, panic, and unreality loom within.
A shiny silver object lies within arm's reach.
A hand moves closer, fingers flex and unflex,
then flex again as the object is grasped in a sweaty palm.
The heft and intent of the instrument are considered, again
and again.
The cloak of blackness grows tighter,
An arm is shakily raised, eyes are closed,
the cold of metal on skin,
An instant of heat..........and all is dissolved.

Beverly Levin Copeland
January 23, 2020.

I would ask myself over and over, "We gave him a good life—then why?" Mike was a real soldier inside and out. He loved his family so much that I knew his pain level must have been unbearable to do this to us. I know he didn't do this to *us*. Again, the whys, ifs, and should-haves that would follow.

I remember trying to make sense of it. But I won't, ever. I still shake my head to this day, thinking about his choice. All kinds of thoughts flashed through my mind. How did this happen? We'd just celebrated Christmas. Mike was great, the happiest we had all seen him.

I remember feeling like I had been in a boxing ring. My head was fuzzy, and the sounds were faded in my head. People were all talking and crying. My daughter mentioned that Mike had come in the night before.

She said he seemed checked out. He went upstairs to my room, and that was the last time she saw him alive.

For the first few weeks afterward, my daughter felt that if she had heard him leave, maybe it would have made a difference. I told her it was not her fault. How many times will we say, *"If," "should have," "could have"* or *"why?"* We cannot stop our loved ones from taking their lives. There are limits to what one can do to stop them. If they want to, they will find a way.

How do I do this? I thought, my mind spiraling. What do I do now? Where do I go? What happens now? I was in shock. It was Christmas week. My life was crumbling like a building rocked by a 9.0 earthquake. Me—someone who was always so strong, one of the things Mike admired about me—*my kids' rock.*

Look at me now, Mike. I was drowning, drowning in the storm. Little did I know what lay ahead....

Chapter Two

Shock and Denial

When Mike first died, I walked around like a zombie, only going through the motions. Then reality would hit me, and I would fall to the floor, sobbing. Everyone's situation is different, of course. Reactions depend on the relationship you had with your loved one. My son and I were very close. Mike was a soldier inside and out. He fiercely loved his family. That is why I know my son must have been in horrific pain to leave us. He knew what it was going to do to us all, but his depression and loss of hope won that morning.

I often went from doing everyday things as if everything was normal, and then reality would hit me again. This habit went on throughout the day for several years and still does. Thank God that I didn't have to work and had some savings. There was no way I would have been emotionally or mentally capable of carrying on a job. The second-year is worse as the fog lifts, and reality hits you. I became severely depressed, losing my desire to stay alive at times. I never tried to take my life, but I did often have passive suicidal ideation. I will speak about both passive and active suicidal ideation in Chapter Four. Life was, and sometimes still is hard.

No matter what anyone said or did, they could not help me. I know people meant well when they would say things like, "Mike wouldn't want you to be sad or to live this way." I would reply in an angry voice,

"Then he shouldn't have taken his life. I don't care what he wants!" People would also say, "But you have another child; Nicole needs you." Please don't ever say that to a parent.

BEFORE YOU TELL A
GRIEVING PARENT TO BE
GRATEFUL FOR THE CHILDREN
THEY HAVE,
THINK ABOUT WHICH ONE OF YOURS
YOU COULD LIVE WITHOUT

Saying things like this to me might seem appropriate to friends and loved ones, but the truth is, my daughter cannot replace Mike. No one can replace another person. Nothing anyone can say or do will make the pain go away. I wish people would understand that it's best to say nothing. Take all the time you need to heal, no matter what anybody says. Anyone who told me that I should get over it by now is not capable of understanding the reality of what's happened to me. I no longer want them in my life, and many aren't. You will tend to tolerate less than you did previously. The actual colors of people in your life become apparent. Good *and* bad. I have fewer people in my life today, but those are the ones I've chosen to be there.

As his mother who gave him life, I'm devastated that he felt that was the only way out. He'd never asked for help. He'd never given me a chance to try and help. It was excruciatingly painful. I took on the pain from others who loved him, too. It was awful for me to picture in my mind my daughter collapsing, her face turning green when her dad had told her the dreadful news, their father seeing the police and the yellow tape, and to also know I wasn't there with her. She would never have her brother around again. My family and his friends were so devastated.

I would sit out in my yard every morning and drink my coffee, crying and talking out loud to Mike. "Mike, look at me. Was it worth it? Do you hear me, Mike? Are you happy? Give me a sign that you hear me." Memorial weekend, on Sunday, five months after Mike died, I was beside myself, exhausted from crying and getting no sleep. My son was a veteran, so I'd heard from many people that said they were thinking of me. The next morning, Memorial Day, I was getting calls asking if I'd seen the newspaper. "I don't get the newspaper anymore since the internet," I'd replied. They asked me to get one. On the front page of the local paper was a tribute to all the veterans. The whole front page was a picture of the Veterans Memorial Cemetery, where my dad and Mike are laid to rest. Inside, the article covered several more pages. On one page is a photo of buried soldiers. Out of all the rows, they could have taken a picture of was my son.

Everyone called him "Kiss" as his last name was Kissell. What are the odds that his row would be in that photo? All you can see is the word *KISS*. I just stared at it, getting goosebumps. I took that as a sign he'd heard me. Photos, below.

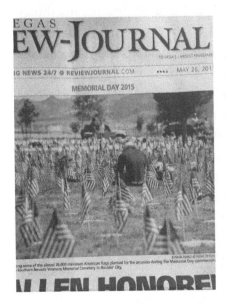

As I sat outside, talking to Mike, looking at my flowers—I've always loved flowers in my yard—the sun shining, all I saw was black and gray. There were no colors, nothing pretty. No beautiful sunsets, no sounds of birds singing. I saw and heard nothing. That's what death and depression can do to a person and their outlook on life. I didn't care how I looked. I showered every day, but I didn't care about anything else. I'd be walking through the grocery store, and suddenly, the thought, *Mike's dead,* would surge to the forefront of my mind. The gut-wrenching reality would hit me. At that moment, I was disabled. Sometimes, I would leave the basket and run out of the store. I'd hold back the tears. I'd continue to move on through the store with my shopping. The store clerk would say, "Smile, it can't be that bad." (I could cry when I got in the car) I could barely talk.

I started going through his clothes, books, movies (over two thousand)! And CDs. I don't know how I did it some days, but I'm glad I did it while I was in shock as I can tell you, I think I would have gone insane seeing everything had I waited. The hardest to endure was coming across photos of him as a child and his military things. I would start crying and go into the house. I let Steve go through his things first, then let my two nephews and his friends go through all Mike's clothes and take out things I didn't need or want to keep. I also gave to specific individuals the things that Mike had wanted them to have. Who has a will at thirty? Next, I took the rest of Mike's things to the homeless area. Mike had a lot of nice clothes, jackets, and boots. It was January. They'd been running down the street when I pulled up to the curb, so happy and thankful. I was glad I could help them, and I know Mike would have been too. I know if he had still been living at home when it happened, I would have shut the door to his room and not looked in there for years, not touching a thing. I still have a hard time throwing away some of Mike's things that don't even work anymore, like his Roku. I feel like I'm throwing *him* away.

I didn't know how I was going to go on. I remember thinking, *God, I have a long life to live without him.* I don't want to live without him.

I was fifty-seven. It was unbearable to even think about it. For so many years, Mike was my comedy partner, my fine-dining partner, my laughter, my first child, my only son. My mantra was, *Dear God, help me; I can't do this anymore.* Then people would remind me I have a daughter—somehow, I had forgotten. I love my daughter; I was overcome by grief over the loss of my son. Nicole was away at college in Southern California, so she wasn't around to remind me. Then I would feel even more depressed that my daughter had a mother like me, completely lost, depressed, and wilting away. Not the strong person she was used to—the glue of our family.

I would tell her how sorry I was that I wasn't emotionally available for her. Of course, she didn't fault me, but I just felt like a bad mother. Every morning when I would wake up, I was disappointed that I was still alive. I went on like this for a good twenty-two months. Going into the second year was the worst. Everyone went on with their lives but me. It does not end after the funeral as most people think; it's just the beginning of a long road. My life, as I knew it, was destroyed—my life would never be the same. Alone, as far as my home went. It was empty, and I was empty. There was a hole in my family. Every family gathering, every holiday, birthdays, Mother's Day, Mike's birthday, Christmas—Mike was gone.

Christmas. At one time, it was my favorite, but it was now the worst holiday for me. Just two days later loomed the anniversary of my son's suicide. How do I enjoy the holidays? The pain and loss were so palpable. The emptiness without him. The unspoken words that everyone was feeling. The empty chair at the table where Mike used to sit. Each holiday a constant reminder that he was gone. I grieved beyond words. A lot of my emotions were internal, so no one knew what I was feeling besides the obvious. There is a sadness inside of me that never leaves. Very few understood except one friend who had lost her son years ago and later, her grandson, who'd taken his life in 2018. She cries all the time. It's such a lonely place to be.

I wished my dad was still around. He died five years before Mike did. He was my go-to person, my biggest cheerleader, the best dad, and grandfather. The kids just loved him; all kids loved him. All three of us were peas in a pod. The two most important men in my life were gone. Both were drop-dead funny, and we laughed so much. Who do I go to now? When I thought of how both of them were gone, my stomach would sink, and I would just lay on my bed and cry. It took me almost five years to recover from the unexpected death of my father. Now Mike was gone. Even now, the memories and feelings when my father died, take me back to that place for a moment. I feel that deep grief and cry while writing this book. I love deeply and am very sentimental and nostalgic.

When a person has had trauma in their life, they most likely will feel that same feeling again, even for a fleeting moment, when they think of that day. It never entirely goes away. I describe it like a scab that never stops bleeding. There are many days that scab gets picked.

The Seven Stages of Grief
(based on the Kubler-Ross Model)

Shock: Initial paralysis at hearing the bad news

Denial: Trying to avoid the inevitable

Anger: Frustrated outpouring of bottled-up emotion

Bargaining: Seeking in vain for a way out

Depression: Final realization of the inevitable

Testing: Seeking realistic solutions

Acceptance: Finally finding the way forward

The seven stages of grief do not necessarily always happen in the same order or for the same length of time. Getting through the first six stages is the grief work that needs to be done until you get to the acceptance stage. I'm not even close to accepting my son's choice or even that he died, at times. I go back and forth between many of these stages.

Denial lasts for however long it takes for the survivor to believe the reality. Of course, the sooner you can come to terms with the death, the faster you will heal. I stumbled around my home most of the time in shock, sometimes too incoherent to speak with family and others who called. Some days I was unable to do anything but cry.

I had to log in to my son's Facebook account to write the terrible news for all his friends and loved ones regarding his memorial service. I could not keep repeating the story to each person that called. I cried and cried all day, every day. I couldn't eat and was terrified to go to sleep as the silence and darkness just made me think of what had just happened, bringing on the panic attacks, and waking up with the reality hitting me that Mike was gone, forever. To this day, I still cannot sleep in silence and hate the darkness. That stabbing, drop in your stomach feeling when reality would hit me again. Mike's family and friends flew in from all around the country for his memorial. Mike had a lot of friends, military friends, and family.

I remember picking out Mike's urn for his cremation, sitting there with his dad, his dad's wife, and my husband at the time. Shaking my head, I asked, "Am I doing this for Mike?" I thought, *how did he die before me?* I started to cry again. They'd asked if I wanted a lock of his hair and his fingerprints, of course. I have a tin box with all his personal belongings in it, even his SIM card from his cell phone on which I will always have all the text messages between us, actually from everyone. I keep it hidden away, so seeing it won't create a trigger. For those that suffer from depression, triggers can set off terrible sadness. For me, the triggers are everywhere. I have to work hard to try and avoid them.

I did not have a funeral for Mike, as he wanted his ashes spread over Lake Tahoe, where he was born, so we held a memorial on January 6—another day, that is a trigger. The memorial was in the chapel at the Veterans Memorial Cemetery. Over three hundred came, standing room only out the door, so we opened the partition from the other side. Our room only held about one hundred. I was overwhelmed with how many people had come—a testament to how many people loved him. Some told me they'd only known Mike for thirty minutes, but he'd made such a memorable impression on them. We laid his military uniform, shoes, and photo upfront on the table with his urn. I'd never realized how heavy a cremated body would be.

His friends had put together a collage of Mike that played on a screen along with music from Frank Sinatra, Michael Bublé, and others. I couldn't even look at them. I couldn't believe I was sitting there for *MY* son. I started to cry again. "You weren't supposed to die before me, Mike. Why couldn't you love yourself as much as everyone here does?" When they played "Taps" folded and gave me the flag, I wailed so loud that it sounded like the cry of an animal that had been bludgeoned to death. That's how I felt, almost falling to my knees. We decided later to bury Mike's ashes near my dad at the Veterans Memorial Cemetery as I did not want him so far from us. We buried Mike the following month, on February 27. He died on December 27. I never look at the number 27 the same way, ever again.

I could have purchased a recorded copy of the service but didn't know that at the time, I wasn't thinking clearly. Looking back, I wish I had bought the video that is recorded. I don't remember much from that day; I was a zombie.

Denial. During most of the first five weeks, I was a zombie. I'd thought Mike was at his apartment and blocked out his death. I said to myself, "He didn't take his life." I received calls, and people came by to keep me occupied instead of thinking so much. I had remarried and was in my sixth month of marriage at the time Mike took his life. I knew I needed help. I didn't know how to handle it or where to go from there, and neither did Bill. He had three sons. Losing a child, especially to suicide, doesn't come with instructions.

Thank God I was proactive because no one could help or knew how. They all meant well. But I was really on my own. No one around me had ever experienced this kind of death or the loss of a child to suicide. On top of that, I was clinically depressed but didn't know it yet. If you're not very careful, it can be easy to escape through alcohol, food binging, under-eating, gambling, drugs, and overspending. If you just don't feel like yourself for whatever reason, I urge you to please seek help. If you are experiencing loss due to suicide, this type of loss is greater than many people know; no matter how strong you think you are, you cannot do this alone.

People who aren't suffering from depression cannot understand why someone who is doesn't just get up, go out and do something and simply—shake it off. It is not that simple. Untreated clinical depression is not simple at all. Those that suffer don't wake up choosing to be depressed that day or any day. It is a very complex and serious illness. Suicide, mental illness, and addictions are the only disease that gets blamed on the person suffering. Do we blame people who have cancer? Or say, "It's just cancer; get over it?" I will speak about this in-depth in another chapter. Untreated depression is the number one cause of suicide (Suicide.org). Despite all the people I had around me, I felt and was very alone.

Unlike many, I did reach out online and searched for support groups, desperate for anyone to help me. I scoured many sites about suicide and depression. Losing Mike caused a tsunami of devastation. Some can find hope, support, and connection through various groups. They have been accommodating for so many, yet none of them stood out to me for the kind of help I needed. A lot of the sites were kind of generic, listing grief counselors, PhDs, etc. Some pages had so much information that it was overwhelming. My head wanted to explode, trying to read all of it, and I would just find another website—they were all bleak and depressing. I needed someone who would understand this devastating loss and somehow try to find something, anything that I could latch onto to save me from drowning. That is why I am telling you about my experiences. I hope something here shouts out to you. Support groups may be all you need, but with clinical depression, it will not be enough to help you. I want to help provide some direction for you based upon my journey and observations. Speaking with someone who has walked in your shoes to some extent can be very helpful and comforting.

I called my church, who gave me the name of two women that have a support group. One of them, Patti, was also a hospice chaplain. I attended for a few weeks. Very nice women. Most support groups don't cost anything. The situations of members of this group varied; not all had lost a child. Most had lost a spouse. I think being involved in it made me get out of the house, which was good. I knew I still needed professional help.

I went to Compassionate Friends, a non-profit support group for parents who had experienced the loss of a child. They meet once a month. I thought maybe hearing their stories and how they were getting through it might help.

I did not return because I knew I needed much more help than they could give me, but for many, it's beneficial. It's good to be around people that can relate to you about the death of a child. Support groups for suicide-loss survivors only are also available. Please visit https://suicidepreventionlifeline.org. They have a wealth of information about where to start.

I knew this was going to be a long, dark road. I just didn't know how long or how dark. I was on welfare and a single mom when I'd had Mike. He was so very special to me, which made the grief worse. I hadn't seen any signs that he was suicidal; there had been no warning. He was the happiest we had ever seen him, and it was Christmas week. Everyone was celebrating.

Looking back now, I realize I'd seen the signs in his short temper and impatience with most things when he came back from his second deployment from Iraq in 2011. Those can be some of the symptoms of depression and PTSD, which I didn't know about then. Like I mentioned, he'd never dealt with his depression and all his compounded grief.

At times throughout the day, the reality would seep in, but my mind would push it away as the truth was too painful to accept. Acceptance is the last stage of grief. I'm not even close to that stage even after five years. Losing a loved one to suicide is a devastating and traumatic experience.

The shock to my system made my recovery worse. What makes suicide loss so unique? Loss by suicide "is distinct from other types of loss in three significant ways: the thematic content of the grief, the social processes surrounding the survivor, and the impact that suicide has on the family systems...The perceived intentionality and preventability of a suicide death, as well as its stigmatized and traumatic nature, differentiate it from other types of traumatic loss. These elements are all likely to affect the nature, intensity, and duration of the grief." (Gutin, NJ, 2018)

No one is prepared to bury their child. I carry a lot of guilt. To this day, it still affects me hearing in my mind Mike's sobs when I'd told him Pop died. They were extremely close. Mike would say to me that his biggest fear, while he was in Iraq, was that Pop would die before he got to see him. My dad had died on the same day as Mike's flight home from his first deployment in Iraq in 2009. I was in shock and beside myself with grief between losing my father and knowing I had to greet my son with that news! I dreaded telling Mike, knowing he was so excited to come home. I cried for the loss of my father but was happy; Mike was coming home. An awful contradiction of feelings. He deserved a better homecoming than that. That bothers me to this day. On his second return from deployment in 2011, I made sure to be there to greet him at Fort Hood to celebrate the homecoming he hadn't gotten the first time.

Now, both are gone. My son took his life at the cemetery. Now both are buried there. I see the picture of Mike's dead body in his truck with a bullet in his head in my mind every time I go there. I see the yellow tape.

I looked for a therapist to see. I knew I needed to speak to someone who could help me through this nightmare. I wanted a Christian therapist. I found a wonderful man who was a pastor and experienced in addressing grief, which was very important. Shopping around and finding someone who specializes in grief counseling—especially in suicide and depression —whom you can connect with is crucial. Many are only marriage and family counselors. A therapist without full knowledge of suicide and its aftermath or mental illness may not be the right fit and could make clinical errors, which could hamper treatment. A clinician is someone who is in the clinical practice (involving direct observation of the patient) of medicine, psychiatry, or psychology as distinguished from one specializing in laboratory or research techniques or theory. Therapists cannot write prescriptions— only psychiatrists or medical doctors can. Today, psychiatrists do not sit with you to have therapy sessions; they only monitor your medication. So, I see both my therapist and my psychiatrist.

I started seeing James, my therapist, right away, and once a week. Many do not accept medical insurance, so ask whether they will discount sessions if you come once a week. Most will. Bill, my husband at the time, only came with me to a session once.

James warned me, "This will be the hardest work you will ever do." Grief work, it's called. I thought, *Work, what work?* James said that a person must deal with the reality and the stages of grief to get to the other side and become healthy, find happiness, and come to terms with the death of their loved one. Everyone grieves differently in their way—there is no right or wrong. But he also said, "If you don't do the work now, it will be harder later on." If you only take away one thing from my writing, take this to heart: don't give up and do the work as soon as you can. I was open to whatever would help me through this nightmare. I was desperate.

James asked me to buy specific workbooks to fill out. He directed me to keep a journal to see how far I'd had come. I can see it when I look back and read it. It did help me to see where my mind was then and now. I did and still do plenty of crying each time I review my journey. He was very sympathetic to what I was going through. He wanted a timeline of my life of good and bad times that had affected me the most—just the year and what had happened. Above the line, I wrote the good times I remembered, and below the line, the bad times that had affected me along with the year it had taken place. Even if it was about my dog dying, he wanted everything that I could remember. It helped him get a picture of my life quicker than through months of therapy. I had never done that before or read about anyone doing that. It was interesting to see how much grief there had been over the years; my sadness outweighed my happiness. He asked me how my relationship was with my mom and asked for one memory that I enjoyed with her that I could remember. Sadly, I couldn't remember many that were memorable in a loving way between her and me.

Don't get me wrong; my mom was as loving as she knew how to be. She spent most of her time cleaning the house; she loved cleaning. At 88, she suffered from sundowner's syndrome and Pick's disease (types of dementia) and passed away in January 2020 while I was writing this book. I have to tell you, being back at the cemetery where my son took his life and is buried, affected me greatly. Death, period affects me. It was a trigger all over again. The same-sex parent is the most important however, I'd always been closer to my dad. Try this timeline exercise; you may be shocked at what you see. It may help you understand what underlying issue/issues may be what is affecting you that you may have suppressed. Mine was a great road map for looking at happy and sad times in my life over the years. That is where healing starts for compounded grief that needs to be your focus.

The stages of grief don't occur in any particular sequence. You may go from one to another and back again to the one you already went through. So many questions arise with suicide that it can make it harder to get through. Some questions buried with your loved one. Many of my family members and his friends were angry at what he did. I was not angry. Yes, that has increased as time goes by, and my journey into grieving continues. I was saddened and overwhelmed by his death, and as his mother who gave him life, the thought that he felt he had to take his life to be happy made me inconsolable at times.

I was deeply in pain as I began to understand the agony he'd felt throughout the night before he made his choice. I still am, and just can't come to terms with that yet. When I think of it, I immediately think of something else—feeling his pain as I'd read his text. I understood most of what he thought as I went into my deep depression from his suicide. He'd never given me or anyone a chance to help him, which made it worse. That fact plays over and over in my mind. We always want our children to be happy. "Look at me, Mike, look at my life now. Was it worth it, Mike?" I'd keep asking. "Are you happy?"

Into the darkness, I went.

Chapter Three

Into the Darkness

A lot can happen in nine months. You can start and grow a business or give birth to a child. It took nine months for me to lose just about everything.

My son's suicide had just backhanded me, followed by a text six months later in June 2015 from my husband, Bill, while I was away with my daughter, telling me he was leaving our marriage. I'd tried calling, but he wouldn't pick up. "You couldn't have picked a worse time," I told him when I got home. He said, "Is there ever a good time?" I broke down. God no, not another loss.

One day he'd told me, "You're not yourself anymore." *What?* I'd thought.

"Of course, I'm not myself—my son just took his life!" I'd screamed. He mentioned that to our counselor in one of my sessions. My counselor's mouth had dropped open. Then he'd told my husband, "She will never be that person again." What kind of a person would say that to their spouse? What kind of a person leaves their spouse by text message six months after their spouse's child dies? What happened to "for better or worse?" To this day, I have nothing good to say about him; he was a very selfish man his whole life. I'm not angry or bitter, I'm indifferent—but I'm honest.

Six months after my son had taken his life, I had to pack and move out of my home with only three weeks' notice. My daughter helped me pack the house up, and a few of Mike's best friends helped me move. I had to abandon a career I'd loved for over ten years that had paid me very well. I had a mental breakdown on July 9—the first of two in four months. I had to move out of my home by July 13. Two months later, I had a full hip replacement. I was mentally and physically bankrupt. I developed severe clinical depression, post-traumatic stress disorder, passive suicidal ideation, and panic and anxiety disorder.

Panic/anxiety attacks can feel like a hot flush from the bottom of your feet to your head. You may start sweating and feel nauseous, and your heart starts racing. You may be too frozen to move. I would get these several times a week for almost three years. When these happen, take slow deep breaths, in your nose, and out your mouth. Deep breaths help with nausea. Get some fresh air if you can. For me, I had to take a Xanax.

I had hit rock bottom, and, ironically, the thought of death seemed more appealing than the life I was now living. I was barely staying afloat in this storm. My therapist told me that he had seen hundreds of people for different reasons, but not in all his years of practice has he seen one patient suffer every significant loss all at the same time. I was in bad shape. I know my family, including my daughter, were afraid for me. I am not by any means, saying that no one has suffered more catastrophic life-changing events than me. I always tell myself that it could have been even worse.

I did try to bargain with God, saying, "Please, God, bring him back and take me." "Please, Dear Lord, I'll never do x, y, and z anymore!" I would scream and cry out loud. Please understand, my state of mind did not mean that I didn't love my daughter. When someone is in that place mentally, they forget who is around them and anything good in their life. I'd forgotten I had a daughter—she lived away from home. My grief consumed me. I was losing hope, just like Mike had.

My whole life had just blown up. How was I going to do this? How do I go on? I didn't want to live. There is a difference between not wanting to live and having suicidal thoughts. I didn't want to be in this "loss of a child" club. Some mothers I'd spoken to had locked themselves in their room all day and shut out their spouses and entire families. I was mourning my *son's death, a failed marriage, the death of the old me and my past life*, my family that now had a hole in it, *recovering from a hip replacement, and experiencing depression*. It was a lot to grieve at one time.

A poem I read expressed precisely how I felt and still do.

The "Hole" Family by Beverly Levin Copeland

My family has a hole in it.

My "whole" family has a hole-a large gaping hole.

No one can fill the hole.

No one can enter that void.

No one in my "whole" family.

My "whole "family goes on,

My "whole" family goes forward.

We struggle to remain whole.

But the hole remains.

Sometimes the hole pulls us closer together,

Sometimes the hole separates us.

Can our arms embracing each other diminish the hole?

When someone says, "Is your "whole" family here" or "Do you want to take a picture of your "whole" family?

I think to myself, "Can't you see the hole?"

No matter what we are doing or celebrating, Mike is not there, I'm reminded, which opens up the wound all over again. I would cry and smell my son's pillow that was found from behind the seat of his truck. I will never wash it, nor the fleece light jacket that I'd bought him that he'd always worn before his death. Those things have become priceless. I can't say enough that deaths from suicide are some of the hardest to understand and accept.

No one could give me what I wanted, which was to have my son back. Most days, I would get dressed, cook, like nothing had happened. I'd think *I have years to live without my son.* Every day was another day without him and a terrible struggle. I would suppress it. I would suppress a lot of things I thought about him, every moment of his life that would creep in. The memories of thirty years were so harrowing. When we were still married, my ex hated when the phone rang for me as I would start crying all over again. I shake my head when I think about it. Even during that horrific time, it had been about him. As my therapist put it, "When God passed out, empathy, Bill didn't get any." Some people are born without it.

In March 2015, I started a Facebook page in memory of Mike, called Suicide: unofficial. I couldn't say it was official as it wasn't a business. I started to speak about my son's suicide in hopes that others might change their mind after hearing about the tsunami of devastation it causes to survivors. It was also a way for me to speak with Mike and tell my story. I felt he'd see my writing when I went on Facebook. I've been very brutally honest. I've held nothing back about the state

I was in, mentally, and emotionally. I also wanted to stay in touch with Mike's friends.

It was probably way too soon for me to go on Facebook. I would cry while posting and sometimes couldn't go on for weeks. I felt even more depressed. I would receive private messages from people saying how brave I was to be so honest that I had helped them. One gal said that after she'd read how his death affected me, it changed her mind, and she reached out for help because she did not want to cause her mom that kind of pain. Those comments kept me going, knowing I'd helped someone. I understood the need to be heard, listened to, and understood by another person. It fulfilled me to be that person for someone else in need. You will find that when you are grieving about the loss of anything, reaching out to help someone else is excellent therapy.

When I created my website, Aftermathofsuicide.com, I changed my Facebook page from Suicide: unofficial to AftermathofSuicide and wrote this book to help make a difference. A single word or post might make a difference in someone deciding to stay alive. I will not allow Mike to have died in this way without a legacy. My story needs to be told, no matter how painful. I had read just about every book on suicide and the death of a child that I could find. There was nothing that resonated with all the losses I had experienced at the same time. Nothing. When I would start thinking about it, I would get panic attacks.

At support groups and in most of the books I read, they told me after several months; most people would stop reaching out. I didn't think they would—not *my* friends and family. But that was correct. Now I hear from very few of those who'd supported me early on, including my family. Sad, isn't it? Many don't know what to say. They don't need to say anything but listen and let me cry and talk about Mike. Many stopped calling—it's not their life. But that's not an excuse. Supporting me should not be about *their* feelings, but help with grieving. For the parents who've lost their child, grieving doesn't stop after the funeral. It's only the beginning of a lifelong, painful journey. Suicide loss is so foreign to most people.

My daughter helped me pack the house up, and a few of Mike's best friends helped me move. Thank you, Nick, Joe, and Nicole. I put everything from the house in storage.

I had my first breakdown on July 9, 2015. I was hospitalized and placed in a seventy-two-hour assessment along with drug addicts, etc. "I don't belong here!" I said. I was asked at the ER if I owned a gun or had pills at home. I said, yes. Because of that, I was a danger to myself even though I had not threatened to kill myself. Many people had pills and guns in their homes, as Nevada is a concealed-carry state. My daughter flew back from Los Angeles. It was very hard on her to see me that way; not only had she lost her brother but at the same time needed to fly back and forth because of my condition. She was afraid she'd lose me too.

My room was empty except for a bed and an end table. The bathroom had a shower but no curtain. I wore a hospital gown and could have a book if I wanted one. No cell phones were allowed, but there were phones in the hall on the wall that was outbound calls only. Patients shared a room with a person of the same gender. There was a room with one TV for everyone to share. We lined up for each meal. They told us when we could eat, have a smoke break, although I didn't smoke. Everything was controlled. I sat in my corner and watched. We were allowed visitors on Saturdays only, one person at a time, who could visit for fifteen minutes each. I happened to be there on a Saturday, so my sister, daughter, and mom came to see me. I was scared to death that someone would suffocate me while I slept. *How can this be my life?* I asked myself countless times.

In there, I felt afraid, which was not helpful. Soon, I'd learn I suffered from PTSD from the shock and trauma caused by my son's suicide. I was discharged on the twelfth, then had to move out of my home on the thirteenth. I had to beg the doctor at the hospital to let me go home

29

a day early. The doctor knew I did not belong there. He did, however, put me on a much better anti-depressant with more dopamine (a happy hormone) in it, which worked much better for me. You'll need to talk about medication with your clinician. I wouldn't suggest accepting medicine from anyone, especially if you have a history of substance abuse.

I will never forget how stressful it was to be there, although the staff was very friendly. Looking back at the experience makes me appreciate my life. Maybe many of you know what I'm talking about if you've been in this type of treatment. Many of the other patients had been in there several times. Cutting themselves, drug-addicted—some had threatened to kill themselves just to stay there. They'd told me it was better for them in there than outside; at least they were getting three meals and a bed. Good God.

Once I moved out, my emotional support companions—Brutus, my Pomeranian, and Sweet Pea, my silky toy poodle, both ten years old—and I moved into my sister and brother in-law's place. My mother was already living there along with my nephew Chris who had one year left in high school. Luckily, it was a big home. Still, there I was, a grown woman living out of a suitcase, losing just about everything. How had my life gotten this way?

Why am I telling you all this? So, you know that *YOU* can make it through, no matter the situation: depression, PTSD, poor living conditions, immense loss, etc. You are important! You matter! You may be depressed, but your depression does NOT define you.

I'd lost everyone except my daughter. I did not want her to go anywhere outside due to fear of losing her too. During the first few months, I was always in a panic when she went out. Please, God, don't take her from me!

Two months later, into living with my sister, I needed a full hip replacement. I thought, "Oh my God." I felt like such a burden to everyone. I would cry every night into my pillow to muffle the sound so no one could hear me. Please, God, don't wake me up! I spent most of my time in my room with my two dogs. As much as I appreciated staying at my sister's home, I hated my life. I'd had my own home since my twenties. They did not understand depression as no one in my family suffered from it, yet they were also grieving from Mike's death. He'd been very close to my sister, who was his godmother. It had been an enormous loss to her sons too. My sister's two boys were like brothers to Mike.

It was just a shock to us all, so heartbreaking. The people I wanted to go to were grieving themselves, which made me feel even more alone, and I knew to see me grieving did not help them. We couldn't even help each other. In fact, according to save.org, every suicide affects one hundred fifteen individuals in the deceased person's circle. It would probably not have been a good thing for my daughter to have seen me that way.

My dogs were small and very well behaved. I did not want to ask my mom or sister to watch them, so I rarely met friends for coffee, etc. I felt that would be yet another thing to ask of them, and as I mentioned, I'd felt like a burden. I was a hermit, which was not what I needed to get well. I begged God to let me die over and over (an example of passive suicidal ideation—more on that in Chapter Four). I only left the house to see my therapist once a week.

I was withering away, physically, and mentally. I weighed only 109 pounds. In my mind, I couldn't see a way out of it all. My mind tangled with darkness, loneliness, grief, and the absence of hope. Losing hope is dangerous. Usually, losing hope is what pushes people over the edge. Later, as I began to study human behavior, mental illness, and suicide, I started gaining an inkling of how difficult and painful that choice had been for my son. The common goal of suicide is to end the pain—not to die. My depression engulfed me.

Chapter Four

Understanding Depression, Post-Traumatic Stress Disorder and Mental Health Conditions Seen in Childhood

"SUICIDAL VS. SUICIDE"

When someone ends up committing suicide, everyone is there; they feel inadequate, they didn't "see the signs" they talk about how amazing you were, and so forth. But if you tell someone you're suicidal; everything is different, no one wants to solve the problem, as a matter of fact, half of the time they act like it isn't a problem, that you won't ever "do it" that it'll just "go away." They treat it like a joke. Well, let me tell you something, being suicidal is no joke, people do consider it as an only option, and treating the problem like it doesn't matter will not get you anywhere, the only place it's going to get you is to a funeral. If someone tells you they're suicidal, don't push them away; instead, try to be the one to keep them here.

In July 2015, I'd reached the first of several rock bottoms. I had hit the wall of severe depression. I was diagnosed with MDD, major depressive disorder, PSTD, post-traumatic stress disorder, and panic/anxiety disorder. The depression I had was not situational depression, which everyone suffers with at some point in their life. It was clinical depression which lasts for a month or longer. Comparing sadness with depression is like saying getting wet is the same thing as drowning.

Your symptoms may also indicate other mental illnesses or disorders, such as manic-depressive disorder (also called bipolar disorder), schizophrenia, psychosis, mania, neurotic stress disorder, major depressive disorder, and many more. If you have not seen a clinician yet, you may find it very helpful. Ask them if they are familiar with suicide loss, depression, or PTSD. Depression left untreated can be devastating and, in many cases, may result in your death. Many people can and do get better. Do not become a victim through self-sabotage. Remaining a victim will not help you and will get you nowhere fast, except the cemetery. Visiting a clinician was one of the things I did for myself that kept me alive. Thank God I was proactive. Please be proactive. **No one** should be more important to you than you! It's brave to ask for help.

Researchers "found that the higher the level of 'perceived closeness' to the deceased, the more likely that survivors of suicide loss would experience PTSD symptoms. Also, the dramatic decline of social support following a suicide loss may itself be traumatic, which can serve to compound these difficulties" (Gutin, NJ, 2018). They also discovered that "many of their clinicians did not assess or diagnose this disorder, missing an important component for treatment." I couldn't concur more.

In fact, "It is important to note that suicidal ideation is not uncommon and can serve different functions for survivors and suicide loss without necessarily progressing to a plan...Survivors... may wish to 'join' their loved one; to understand or identify with the mental state of the deceased; to punish themselves for failing to prevent the suicide, or to end their pain through death" (Gutin, NJ, 2018).

Myths About Suicide

***Myth*:** People who talk about taking their own lives just want attention.

Fact: Most people who consider suicide do talk about it. My son did not. If someone is talking about how it would be better if they weren't here or being in distress or symptoms of depression, please ask them if they are suicidal. If so, please call the crisis line at 1-800-273-8255. The signs of depression are not always the ones most people think of, i.e., sadness, loss of interest., Etc. Often symptoms include anger and agitation.

Myth: Asking a person if they are suicidal may give them the idea to do it.

Fact: No one can make someone think of doing it unless they were already thinking about it. Asking that person, if they are suicidal could bring relief. It lets them know people care.

***Myth*:** People think suicides increase around the holidays during the winter.

Fact: Suicides increase in the spring. That's when most people start becoming more social and go out due to good weather. It hits them that others may want them to get out more as well. They begin to feel pressure and anxiety.

Suicide is the second leading cause of death for Americans aged fifteen to twenty-four (Save.org). And an average of twenty-two US veterans and active service members take their lives each day (US Dept. of Veterans Affairs, 2019). This situation has to change! It is a crisis, and we need to stop the stigma associated with mental illness. How many people know these statistics?

Untreated depression is the number one cause of suicide (Suicide.org, 2019).

Over one million people worldwide take their lives each year (World Health Organization, 2019).

More than 300 million people around the world will experience
a form of depression each year (W.H.O., 2019).
One in four will have a mental disorder (W.H.O., 2019).

According to mayoclinic.org, "Although depression may occur only once during your life, people typically have multiple episodes. During these episodes, symptoms** occur most of the day, nearly every day and may include:

Feelings of *sadness, tearfulness, emptiness* or *hopelessness*

Angry outbursts, irritability or frustration, even over small matters

Loss of interest or pleasure in most or all normal activities, such as sex, hobbies or sports

Sleep disturbances, including *insomnia* or sleeping too much

Tiredness and *lack of energy*, so even small tasks take extra effort

Reduced appetite and *weight loss* or increased cravings for food and weight gain

Anxiety, agitation or restlessness

Slowed thinking, speaking or body movements

Feelings of worthlessness or guilt, fixating on past failures or self-blame

Trouble thinking, concentrating, making decisions and remembering things

Frequent or recurrent thoughts of death, suicidal thoughts, suicide attempts or suicide

Unexplained physical problems, such as back pain or headaches

"For many people with depression, symptoms usually are severe enough to cause noticeable problems in day-to-day activities, such as work, school, social events, or relationships with others. Some people may generally feel miserable or unhappy without really knowing why" (Mayo Clinic, 2019).

**I used bold italics to indicate symptoms on the list my son had. The signs were there, but I did not associate many of them with depression. I didn't know then what I know now. What did we know thirty years ago? I'd never thought a six-year-old could be depressed. But it can happen, and he was.

As a child, some of the symptoms are different. My son would bang his head against the wall until there was a green bump on his forehead. He'd been defiant at times, but I thought, "Boys will be boys." He wasn't unruly in public, so I'd thought he was doing it for attention at home. I did take him to see a counselor when he was young, his diagnosis, defiant disorder.

Of course, after Mike's death, I thought, "If I could just go back and do it over..." which, of course, would start my cycle of depression all over again. The *whys* and *ifs* or past regrets of suicide. I feel there would be nothing worse than dying with regrets.

I dug deep into understanding mental illness and post-traumatic stress disorder. It helped me understand my son's battle and now my own.

Why do I use the words mental illness? Because this condition *is* an illness, just like cancer or multiple sclerosis, but it's invisible, so no one understands or thinks you're ill. They can't see it! Suffering from mental illness is not a failure. Years ago, people were afraid to talk about mental illness because most people would think of movies in which we saw people strapped into straitjackets. People are afraid to speak out and ask for help. It's ok not to be ok; it's *not* ok to *not* ask for help. It's nice to see some entertainers and actors finally talking about it, telling their stories; for example, the actor, Dwayne "The Rock" Johnson; the singer, Demi Lovato; and J. K. Rowling, the author of the Harry Potter books. Johnson suffers from depression and had thoughts of suicide many times. His mother attempted it when he was fifteen. Lovato suffers from manic depression. She has been in and out of rehab several times. See Rowling's comment below. I have such respect for those in the limelight who come out and talk about this painful disease.

"Depression is the most unpleasant thing I have ever experienced…It is that absence of being able to envisage that you will ever be cheerful again. The absence of hope. That very deadened feeling, which is so very different from feeling sad. Sad hurts, but it's a good feeling. It is a necessary thing to feel. Depression is very different." (J.K. Rowling) A 2014 article in *The Sunday Times* reported on how J. K. Rowling spoke about her depression. She admitted that she had contemplated suicide and finally sought professional help after something her daughter had said to her. When she had contacted her doctor's office while her usual general practitioner was away, her concerns were dismissed by the replacement doctor. Thankfully, her regular doctor reviewed the notes and called her two weeks later to schedule counseling. "She saved me because I don't think I would have had the guts to go and do it twice," Rowling stated. In an interview for a university student magazine, she said, "I have never been remotely ashamed of having been depressed. Never. What's to be ashamed of? I went through a rough time, and I am quite proud that I got out of that."

In the article, "Mental Health Conditions Seen in Childhood," Dr. Fuller recognized that "our children are often our greatest pride and joy. They are our future. We love them, raise them, teach them, laugh with them, play with them, and nurse them back to health. As protectors, we want to do everything we can to keep our little ones happy and healthy. But unfortunately, genetics, society, and trauma all play a major role in the development of mental health conditions, and children are not exempt. Studies show that 7.7 million youth aged 6-17 experience a mental health disorder each year—that's one out of every six children in the US." For that reason, "it's important to pay close attention to a child's mental health. While abnormal behavior could just be normal aspects of childhood or a phase of growth or puberty, it could also be a mental health disorder" (Fuller, K., 2019).

"A major goal for those who have lost a loved one to suicide is the ability to find and create meaning from the loss...Memorialize and honor the deceased...Treatment for suicide loss survivors suggests that while most participants find it generally helpful, a significant number of others report that their therapists lack knowledge of suicide grief." Also, researchers found "that survivors of suicide loss who endorsed PTSD symptoms were not assessed, diagnosed, or treated for these symptoms. My book speaks to the importance of understanding what is 'normative' for survivors of suicide loss" (Nina J. Gutin, Ph.D., NJ, 2018).

Many survivors don't want to move on. Which is still a hard thing for me to do. We need to learn how to bear the loss instead of people telling us to get over it. I've had to learn that my life is not nor will be the same anymore. I need to accept this new normal, which is not easy. I don't want to move on. It is accepting my son's death, which is the hardest to do. I want my old life, the old me. Many people think that if they accept the new life, it means they don't care about their loved ones anymore. I battled with that and did feel guilty in the beginning. Of course, that is not the case now.

It is crucial to find a clinician that understands suicide grief and the after-effects for the survivors. Ask them if they are familiar with clinical depression, PTSD, etc. Just because you may have any of these, it does not mean you are going crazy or *are crazy*. I was relieved to hear this is normal. Many questions are buried with the one that died. I needed to understand his battle and mine.

I created my website, AftermathofSuicide.com, during the fourth year after Mike's suicide, in memory of my son.

You would think after five years that I would have it more together. Many days, it's easy for something to trigger me, like a picture on Mike's Facebook page, which seemed meaningless at the time but catches my eye and brings me to my knees. I was so profoundly depressed that I could barely gather enough strength to keep myself alive at times. A few family members thought I'd been acting that way for attention. I was chastised with, "Do not do this to your daughter." I could have taken my life that day in September 2016—no one picked up the phone. Take every threat, and people that talk about dying seriously.

I suffer from post-traumatic stress disorder. Some of the symptoms are:

Feeling emotionally cut off from others
Feeling numb or losing interest in things you used to care about
Feeling constantly on guard
Feeling irritated or angry outbursts
Having difficulty sleeping
Having trouble concentrating
Being jumpy or easily startled
Feeling upset by things that remind you of what happened

The trauma of any kind, especially the ones that blindside you, can affect you in many ways. They can damage you for life. PTSD is usually associated with the military, as servicemen and women have experienced some of the worst possible trauma in numerous ways. Any trauma can trigger PTSD. Like combat, sexual abuse, traumatic loss, etc.

The shock from my son's text—I don't even know how to describe the feeling when it came in, and to be told he was found dead when I was hoping for a different outcome—was so traumatic for me. From his text coming in and finding out he was no more was only three and a half hours. We'd just celebrated Christmas two days before! To this day, when I hear of any type of death, I'm taken right back to that place the day my son took his life, and I received the news. My stomach drops, and the fear and the pain are instant.

I know what other suicide loss survivors and anyone who has lost someone are feeling and going through and will go through in the days and months ahead. Death affects me so very much. I don't look at it the same way anymore; it has a whole new meaning of sadness, darkness, and a lonely place. A finality that I didn't think much about before Mike's death.

The depression I had between 2015 and 2016 made those my toughest, hardest years. They say the second year is worse than the first as you're in shock most of the first year. That is absolutely the truth. The fog lifts after the first year. Reality should set in. Amazingly, I hadn't turned to drugs or alcohol. If I can help anyone identify with me or something that I share that helped me, maybe it can be of help to you and save you time and more grief.

So, death is a trigger and sets off my depression. I am not afraid to die, but I would never take my life. No one has a clue about those little things that you go through. Commercials for Disneyland, *Game of Thrones*, the show *The Office*, or Johnnie Walker Blue Label can be triggers for me. Hearing on TV that someone died by suicide is the worst. I internalize a lot of my sadness and pain. I may not show it or say anything, but the pain is always there behind the smile when there is one.

Right now, writing this, I've experienced what I just mentioned. That specific picture that may pop up as a Facebook memory—all of a sudden, it's right smack in your face, unexpectedly, when you're not thinking about it. It could be a picture, a show you're watching, a song that you hear, or a flashback of a memory, a restaurant on a corner. Music by my son's favorite group, Metallica. Every time I visit the cemetery, I play the Metallica song "Nothing Else Matters" for Mike and just sit and cry the whole time. I can even smell my son's cologne in my mind. The touch of his beard on my cheek. These memories and thoughts trigger my PTSD and depression and are called grief attacks.

Depression is a vast topic; many books have been written about just this one word. Some people are depressed and don't even know it because they can go through the motions of working, cooking, taking care of the family, driving, etc. They don't think they're depressed and so it goes untreated. People may say to them, "You might be depressed; you should get yourself checked." They may respond, "I'm okay," but really, they're not okay. Their spouse/partner/child/friend/ parent might tell them, "You're not okay," but they could be in denial, not realizing they're depressed. On top of the denial of suicide, they experience a refusal to go deep into their feelings.

I still see my psychiatrist every few months to check in with her as she wants to hear how I'm doing on my medication, making sure I'm on the right one, or whether maybe I need to add another one to it or change the one I'm on. I know some people are against medication, and that's okay. It saved my life. I also see my therapist, Amy, every week since I moved east in 2016.

My doctor once said, "Denial is not a river in Egypt." There is nothing wrong with reaching out for help. It's brave. It takes a lot of courage to ask for help. Many stay stuck and suffer for years. Most people that suffer from it would love for you to ask them, "Are you ok?" or "Are you suicidal?" If their answer is yes, please ask, "Do you have a plan?" For many, these questions can be lifesaving. They can feel someone cares. It can be the difference between life and death.

I did feel like a burden to my family, especially to my daughter, who was only twenty-five at the time. Many people don't know that depression can come on quick. It's not something a person chooses to have. No one wakes up in the morning and says, "You know what? I want to be depressed today." I am going to keep repeating this: Untreated depression is the number one cause of suicide (Suicide. org). Some people with depression have thought about suicide for many days, months, or years, or they have tried it and failed. They may never have had a diagnosis or treatment. They may not see life getting better and cannot take the pain and loss of hope any longer.

It's important to recognize there are two kinds of suicidal ideation: passive and active. **Passive suicidal ideation** involves wishing you were dead or that you could die, but not having any plans to commit suicide. **Active suicidal ideation,** on the other hand, requires not only thinking about it but intending to commit suicide, including planning how to do it.

If you feel a friend or loved one may be depressed or suicidal, Verywell Mind (https://www.verywellmind.com/) recommends asking them four straightforward questions:

Do you have a history of depression or mental illness?

Are you on medication, and if so, what kind?

How long have you been having thoughts of suicide?

Have you created a suicide plan?

Life is hard, and it's harder when you're not well. I was trying to survive the loss of my son to suicide, not knowing what to do next. I felt alone and remember thinking, *what do I do next, God? Look at my life? Dear God, help me.* I thought my daughter would be better off without me. I was a mess. I would go back and forth between asking God to help me and asking God not to wake me up.

Medication for depression doesn't put you on a straight road right away. If you decide to take medication, doing so has many hills, peaks, and valleys and can sometimes send you straight down at two hundred miles per hour until you're prescribed the right medication. Just know that your clinician will talk with you about what might be best based on your symptoms, situation, and diagnosis, should you decide to take that route. With the way I was feeling, taking medication was worth a try. I was desperate, and it has been a lifesaver.

I was experiencing loneliness, sleep disturbances, agitation, impatience, lack of energy, and headaches, and recovering from a hip replacement. So, on top of the depression, I had all of that *and* the loss of my son. When I'm depressed, I just want to be alone or stay in my room. I know that's the worst thing to do, but I don't want to bring anyone down around me no matter what they say. I've never been one to display fake emotions. I remember asking someone, "I could go out and pretend I'm happy, is that what you want?" I can't fake happiness or fun. I don't want to—it takes too much energy. Being yourself is the *best* thing you can do for you.

You may have to carry on a job, care for your children, care for a spouse, or an elderly parent. I'm grateful actually that I did not have a job at the time, as I was not mentally capable of performing it. I was fortunate to have some savings. I applied for and received Social Security Disability. Not everyone qualifies for it, and it may take months to hear back from them and receive a check. The wait could also add to your depression. I'd asked God, "What did I do so wrong to be punished?" God was not punishing me, but those were my thoughts.

I love and adore my son. His death triggered the worst depression. I still suffer from both depression and post-traumatic stress disorder. It's manageable now, yet I still have my low moments. The pain left behind for those that love the one who's committed suicide was the reason I wrote this book, started a website called AftermathofSuicide. com, and talk about my depression and onset of PTSD since my son's death.

It has gotten better, but I have a long way to go. Some days, it's two steps forward, three steps back, as they say.

If this is how it is for any of you, I can't tell you how sorry I am. I feel your pain.

When the dynamics of your family are ripped apart, it's catastrophic. We are never the same and spend the rest of our lives trying to create a new normal. You may decide not to be a stick in the mud, but you can't stop the heart from wanting what it wants. Some days, we don't give a shit and let the chips fall where they may. And the next day, we try and clean up the mess. I so wish for the old days again; I miss them. Today it is still hard for me to let go of all I have lost.

In September 2017, I received a call from Bill, my ex, asking me to forgive him. He said I was one of the first persons he needed to call. He told me he had cancer. I told him I forgave him as holding a grudge isn't healthy, and I had moved on. A year later, almost to the day, he passed away from liver cancer. I'm not one to eulogize the dead as if once they die, they all of a sudden become exceptional people. We all know some people who do that. He wasn't—not to anyone. He was a very selfish man. Some people have said, "That's Karma for what he's done to so many in his life." Who knows?

Chapter Five

Who Was Mike?

Chapters one and five were the hardest for me to write. Where do I start about someone larger than life? He is much more than someone who took his life and suffered from depression. I don't say this just because he is my son. Everywhere I went, someone knew him, raved about him, and loved him. When my daughter was out of the house, and people heard her last name, they'd always ask if she was Mike's sister. There were people at his memorial who'd only met him for thirty minutes and told me they had to come. I was very touched. He was someone people didn't forget.

He was an old soul who could converse with a ninety-year-old man when he was five. When he walked into a room, everyone was drawn to him. He could speak to anyone about any subject—history, politics, religion. He soaked up information. He loved the History Channel and the Discovery Channel. I always called him my Jedi Knight as he had both a fun and a dark side where the demons lived, like Darth Vader. He loved *Star Wars*, *Game of Thrones*, *Goodfellas*, and *A Bronx Tale*. His favorite movie was *Braveheart*. Mike loved castles and things from medieval times; he always drew them. Although his favorite band was Metallica, he loved all genres as I loved having music on in the house. Mike LOVED video games and was also a movie buff.

He was my comedy partner. We both enjoyed watching comedians perform. I took him to see Robin Williams, Chris Rock, George Carlin, and Dane Cook. He was a Robin Williams fan. If you've ever watched Robin's Scottish golf scene on YouTube, my son did it precisely like that, with the accent and all. It was one of his best skits. He could speak like Donald Duck and would make me laugh so much. He was always joking. Mike's on the right in the photo above.

Mike, Steve, and Nicole

Mike (left) and his chaplain, Josh Remy, who took
his life eleven months before Mike.

Athena, Mike's half-sister

He was meticulous, and everything in his closet was color coordinated. He could draw freehand at four years old, sometimes in 3D. Above is an image he created in his graphics class (he smoked). I'd never noticed the heart-shaped cloud until after he died. Mike and his half-sister, Athena, finally got to know one another for the ten years before

49

Mike died, Athena's the same age as Nicole. He was loved more than he knew. I wish he'd loved himself as much. He was everyone's best friend, which didn't surprise me at all. He was their go-to guy. Mike's best friend, Nick, says they are all lost without him. He was a great human being, a sensitive person, and a soldier inside and out who would do anything for you. Not without complaining, though; he had a big mouth! Mike entertained and prevented so many in the military from taking their lives, but hadn't been able to save himself. Several years before, I remember asking my son why he hadn't gone to the VA to get help. He'd said, "Are you kidding? The wait time is about five weeks, and you never see the same doctor." Wow, I'd thought, that's awful. I'd mentioned that antidepressants worked for a lot of people. He replied, "Those are for pussies." That's what the military teaches them, not to ask for help—to "man up."

Mike was honorably discharged in 2011. As Army Chaplain Assistant, his responsibilities required assisting military families with grief counseling and helping fellow soldiers deal with depression along with other administrative duties for his chaplain. He clearly should not have been in that position. Regrettably, the military administration and chain of command threaten active personnel with loss of rank and status—stripping them of their stars and stripes—for seeking professional, medical, and psychological help. I'd heard this firsthand from other soldiers. Mike's first chaplain had told me the Chief Chaplain in the Army took his life. Only about five hundred chaplains remain in the Army.

Helping veterans after returning from the battlefield who are struggling with depression and post-traumatic stress disorder should not take five weeks! Sadly, as a result, twenty-two veterans take their life each day. Suicide is now up to forty percent. It is a crisis! The government has made it easier for them to get help much quicker due to the rise in suicides, and all of the increased attention mental illness has finally received.

Mike refused any counseling or medication, which I believe would have made a difference. It has for me. I wished he had just tried. Mike had compounded grief that was not addressed. Often, it only takes one more disaster for everything to come crashing down for sufferers, which is what happened to Mike.

Over the years, I had done everything he would allow me to, to get him help for his on-again-off-again depression. He did not want meds. Mike was always the happiest after getting a new toy, a new video game, a new vehicle, etc. The happiness was still short-lived, though. We all know happiness doesn't come from things. Never rely on another person for your joy. Mike needed to love himself instead of depending on someone else for his happiness, as he always had.

When he was young, Mike never seemed to be cheerful for long. He seemed to have an underlying sadness. Mike was diagnosed with defiant disorder when he was around six years old. We had tried medication for him, but I hadn't liked the way it affected him, and I could tell he didn't like it either. Maybe it wasn't the right medication, but thirty years ago, what did we know about depression?

Throughout most of Mike's life, he was very hard on himself and would hate himself when he got angry or said nasty things to his sister or others. He couldn't control what came out of his mouth when he got angry. When Mike was around eight, he told me how he hated himself, but just didn't know how to handle his anger and wished he was more like Nicole, which saddened me so much. I tried everything I could... consulting with every doctor, and followed up on every complaint he had. I was exhausted trying to make him happy. At the same time, I felt such sadness that he was depressed. He had a good family home, a sister, and parents who loved him. A loving Italian family. My parents adored him, and his cousins and aunt (my sister) all loved him so. When someone has a chemical imbalance, love has nothing to do with it.

Mike loved to write comedy. Below is what he wrote in the Army:

The Creed of the Specialist

No one gets away with more than I. I am a non-Non-Commissioned Officer, a beast of burden. As a junior enlisted soldier, I realize that I am a member of an under-appreciated, much-chastised group of soldiers, which is known as the ribcage, or perhaps pancreas, of the Army.

I am proud of myself and my fellow Specialists and will continue to bitch, whine, and sham until the absolute last second regardless of the mission at hand. I will use my grade and position to avoid responsibility, accountability, and any sense of the presence of the mind.

Ignorance is my watchword. My two best excuses will always be on the tip of my tongue, "I didn't know," and "It wasn't me." I will strive to remain invisible and unavailable for details. "Never, ever volunteer for anything," is my rallying cry.

I am aware of my role as an SPC, and if you need me for anything, I'll be on an appointment. I know the other soldiers, and I will always refer to them by their first name or, in some cases, derogatory nickname. On weekends or days off, I will consistently drink myself into oblivion, and I will never answer my phone. I understand that for a person in my hierarchal position, rewards are going to be few and far between, and punishment will always be swift and severe.

Officers of my unit will have maximum time to accomplish their duties because I will be accomplishing it for them. I will kiss up to their face and badmouth them behind their back, just like everyone else. I will be loyal to those with whom I serve, provided there's something in it for me. I am the last bastion of common sense that stands between me and the Army philosophy of "Work

Harder, Not Smarter." My voice is a tool, and my complaints are a weapon that I wield with unmatched skill and finesse. I will not forget, nor will I allow my comrades to forget, Specialist is the greatest rank in the Army, and rank has its privileges.

God, how I miss him. He had sarcastic humor, which was just like mine. We were very much alike, but I was not as intense, nor did I anger as quickly. I'd like to share a few messages I received from Mike's friends and Army buddies after he died.

> Hi, I'm not sure if you remember me or not, I went to Palo Verde and graduated in 2003. I was friends with Mike. I haven't had a Facebook in years and created one yesterday. I went to look up Mike to add him, and that's when I found out what had happened. I'm so sorry. It brought tears to my eyes when I read his page. I moved to Las Vegas in 2001, not knowing anybody. I got a job that summer at Freddie's Car Wash. Mike was the first person I ever met when I moved to Las Vegas. He went out of his way to make sure I had a friend and to introduce me to all the people he knew. We had classes together; we went to parties together, we hung out all the time. For the two years I lived in Las Vegas, 99% of my memories include him. For whatever reason, a memory that I have like it was yesterday was on the first day of school (after knowing him over the summer), we had a class together. I remember he looked down at my Adidas shell-toe shoes, and he was like, "Here, let me see your shoes," and in my head I was like, why would I give you my shoes in the middle of class? But he persuaded me to take them off, so I did and handed them to him. I figured it was going to be a prank or something funny or strange. Well, it turns out I

had laced my shoes laces wrong or not the cool way. While we were supposed to be taking notes, here is Mike redoing my shoelaces so I don't get laughed at or someone points them out, I guess. You know, back then, that was a big deal, and I guess not knowing anyone, and it was the first day of school he was looking out for me. Never in a million years would I have ever thought someone would want to take off my shoes to fix my shoelaces so it looked cooler. He was always there and looking out for me. Lots of fond memories of Mike. Again, I'm truly sorry for your loss; he was such a great guy. The last time I saw him was in 2006 when I went back out to Vegas to visit him for a week. - Kris

Ma'am, I know you're very busy with the arrangements for Mike. I am stationed in Germany and will not be able to attend his memorial. I served with Mike during his deployment with CH Remy. Mike kept me sane during that time and was the center of laughter everywhere he was. I know you are upset the way his life ended, but you raised an incredible man who inspired so many to be great as well. Even though I was a higher rank than Mike and was older than him, I looked up to him for advice because that's the kind of man he was. As I read all the posts on Facebook about him, that's what we all will remember about him. Deeply sorry for your loss and I will keep you and the rest of Mike's family in my prayers. With respect, SSG Brian

Few ppl was as genuinely amazing as him. Miss him all the time. Especially facing all this discrimination bc no lie, he was the person who gassed me up the most and made me start speaking up. I never told him, but his get it attitude and speaking up not down to ppl was what I admired most (minus how sensitive he was bc my god he was so in tune with some shit). It was so fitting he was the Chaplin's assistant. I pray his mother is at some type of peace. She deserves it. (this is exactly how the message was written)

How do you make sense of losing someone you loved to suicide? Especially when that person was a Chaplain's Assistant, doing 'therapy' for Soldiers right alongside you in Iraq?

I had the honor of meeting Mike in 2010 during OIF/OND. It was a 2nd deployment for each of us. We were both originally based out of Ft. Hood, TX; our paths just hadn't crossed until Kirkuk. The Chaplaincy "office" was next door to the Combat Stress Control "office." We spent a lot of time together... him ALWAYS making me laugh, especially. We even hung out after Iraq once we were both back in FHTX.

He was the type of man who would just make you laugh at anything and everything. That would help you work through whatever personal hell you were going through. So, relatable. So, loving. So, genuine.

We saved an incalculable number of lives that deployment. Soldiers who'd, an hour before seeing him or me, had their loaded M-4 in their mouth with their finger on the trigger - ready to go. SO HOW IS IT THAT WE LOST YOU TO THE

VERY THING YOU SPENT YOUR CAREER PREVENTING? Why didn't I see that you were hurting and needed someone? Why didn't I reach out more? How did it come to this, Kiss?

Suicide is so real. The pain left behind is unimaginable. His mom keeps up his FB page and has even started the Aftermath of Suicide (it has its FB page, too). I see her struggle to make sense of this, too.

ELEVEN MONTHS, Michael. That's all it took between Josh (the very Chaplain you were 'responsible' for assisting), and you end your lives. In the same way, no less. This never gets easier. The world lost such a beautiful soul five years ago on this day.

I'm sorry I didn't see your pain. I'd give anything to save you from it. I love you, Kiss. I'm so sorry.

Michael A. Kissell 11.15.84 - 12.27.14

Until Valhalla 💔 Sydney Cox

That was who my son was and so much more. I've received many emails that broke my heart, and I cry when I read them. Between the joy he gave others and the pain I was left with, I don't know whether I was happy or sad to read them.

After Mike died, when his birthday would come around, people would ask me, "What are you doing to celebrate Mike's life?"

I'd say, "Nothing. I'm still grieving my son's death; I can't even think about celebrating his life."

The thought of his birth triggered my depression, thinking how happy that day was. I'm very nostalgic. Still, after five years, I cannot get myself to look at his face in any picture. I have one photo of him up in the living room.

You must do what is right for you, no matter what others tell you. The fourth-year after his death, I made a fried egg sandwich on his birthday. That was one of Mike's favorites. That's the closest I've come to celebrate. Over time, I will remember that Mike's suicide was only a part of him and that there were also many moments of laughter, fun, love, intelligence, and so much more. Right now, it's still too painful to comprehend. When you can begin to switch from grief to memories of the happy times and laughter, you'll know you are healing and progressing. Most days, I'm still not there.

Chapter Six

Moving Forward One Day at a Time

I want to inspire people. I want someone to look at me and say,

"Because of you, I didn't give up."

We could all be that to someone.

My daughter was with me on the first anniversary of Mike's death, which was the hardest. She has always spent that week with me every year since his death. All the firsts are the hardest. It was excruciating to relive every minute, hour, and day during those first few months. I would look at the clock, thinking of that day into the evening and the next and the next. I dread November through December every year. Mike's birthday is on November 15. Christmas was always my favorite holiday. Now I think, *"That day is coming."* Every time I see the number twenty-seven, my mind goes to *that day.*

While everyone else is merry, I'm in pain, but I put on a smile. In the first two years, I didn't even put up a tree. I lived alone in California that first year and I went up to Los Angeles and stayed with my daughter. We cried and cried most of the day as we hugged each other.

During the third year in 2017, when I moved east, I took out the family Christmas decorations to finally put up a tree. As I opened the boxes, I saw the ornaments Mike had made when he was a child in school—the ones that they make with shredded wheat and green dye to make it look like a wreath ornament with a place for their photo in the middle. I dropped to my knees—I was not expecting to see that. I cried and cried.

Moments like this will happen. You can be happy then all of a sudden, you breakdown. As I looked at them, I had to put them on the back of the tree so I couldn't see them, even though I felt guilty. All the memories came back from those days as I was trying to be in the spirit of Christmas. I could not just leave them in the boxes, or I'd feel like I was putting my son in a box. All of Nicole's things were displayed, but not Mike's. When I see something of his, I feel guilty for not putting it up or on the table. I can't look at very many of his things, still.

One of the hardest things to see was the stocking my mother had made when he was born. He'd fit in it—beautiful needlepoint with his name on it. In the storage box, there lies an ornament with a picture of him in the "Baby's First Christmas" stocking. Now I've turned it over, so I won't see it when I open the box before Christmas. Every Christmas, I look at the other stockings and notice Mike's is not there, and sadness overcomes me. People suggested putting it up, but it didn't matter whether it was up or not. Either way, it was a painful reminder.

So many triggers can make depression worse. Mine happen all year long—some months worse than others—and in every city that I went to with Mike. We traveled a lot over the years since he was six weeks old.

I have continued my weekly therapy with Amy since moving east. As you can tell, it has been a slow uphill battle for me. Along with my son's death, I've experienced numerous turbulent occurrences within the first two years, including another hip replacement and a cervical fusion due to a car accident. I used to speak with my therapist about them and say, "If no one knew me, they would not believe all this was happening in my life in such a short period." She agreed. I counted at least seven events on top of my son's death and depression. They're too detailed to go into, but I can say that I cried throughout the first four years and saw my therapist every week. I came to her with one thing after another. She made me feel heard, but also helped me deal with one thing at a time, instead of looking at the whole picture and feeling overwhelmed. Narrowing your focus down to one thing is difficult but very important because it is easy to feel beaten. Handle the most important thing first.

My therapist had worked her way up to Executive Director by the time she left after twenty-five years of working at the crisis center and suicide prevention 24-hour hotline. Her sister had committed suicide. After seeing her for at least a year, I also found out we had the same birthday: February 25. I'd had no idea she worked in that area, nor about her sister. Choosing her had not been a coincidence; I do not believe in coincidences. That word is a mathematical term which means to coincide, to fit exactly.

Here's another coincidence. When I first moved back to New Jersey—after driving across the country in four days, alone—I pulled into my girlfriend's driveway. It was November 15, my son's birthday. I hadn't planned it that way.

I met Joe—who I've been with for over three years—three weeks after I got there. One night, when I went to his place after we'd first started dating, I noticed a "Save the Date" card on his fridge. His son got married on my son's birthday, November 15, and his daughter-in-law's name is Nicole (my daughter's name). Joe's mother and mine have the same birthday. Coincidence?

Joe is my lifesaver, and the best relationship I have ever had. He makes me laugh so much. He loves me, my daughter, and my dogs unconditionally. I haven't experienced love like that since my dad was alive. I was missing that in my life. He is so much like my dad and son. They both have made me laugh so much and are the funniest people I had ever been around. Laughter is huge to me, and we are both Italian and understand each other's culture. Three years ago, I would have never thought that I would laugh and be happy again. I know Mike sent me to meet Joe. Back in 2007, I moved east temporarily to help open a new resort for Hilton in New York City. I was only planning on being there for a few years. He was in Iraq at the time, and my daughter was eighteen. He'd bitched about me leaving the family. I loved it here but moved back as I felt guilty. I'm glad I did because that gave me four more years with my son. He knew how much I loved it, so I know he sent me back here to meet Joe.

Joe is also a life coach, web site; clearpaththinking.com and author of, "Don't Believe Everything You Think" which you can order at my web site, AftermathofSuicide.com, on the "Meet Jill" page or on his web site.

His path involves helping people with situational challenges that can lead to temporary depression, and I'm focused on helping people with clinical depression. We learn from each other.

I've lived the first four years—and still do—in the past, not wanting to let go. I live with the memories and happy times and days gone by when everyone was alive. I yearn for that life. Saying part of me died with my son is an understatement. I grieve the part of me that died with him. I had a great childhood in an Italian family, full of love and food. It's a running joke with me: Italians either hug you, feed you, or kill you.

Many don't want to let go of their loved ones. The reason so many live in the past and do not want to move forward. Guilt can be associated with the thought of "moving on" from your loved one because living in the past is a way of staying connected. I *still* don't want to let go. It is very normal to feel that way.

You will grieve for many things that have died with your loved one. Allow yourself to feel what you feel. If you feel suicidal, please tell someone. If you know someone who might be suicidal, please ask them directly, "How can I help you?" which makes them feel you care.

Lifeline 1-800-273-8255 (USA only)

When someone dies, people often speak of finding closure. What does that mean anyway? When I hear the word, I always think, *how do you find closure after losing a child?* And not from death by natural causes—not that losing a child in any way is easy—but because he shot himself in the head with a gun? How do you comprehend that? How can one put a gun to their head and pull the trigger? Thinking about it, I shiver as I shake my head again. I can't believe he did it. I cry, "Oh God, Mike, I want to redo the ending. I want to bring you back. All my questions buried with you."

Certain friends will quietly move on since the old you are gone.

Chapter Seven

Living Again and Final Thoughts

You may have unrealistic or possibly no expectations. Don't put any pressure on yourself or let anyone else. At times, you will be down, and other days, the sun will be shining brightly enough for you to begin to see it; life can and likely will be a roller coaster. I know you're probably thinking, "I won't ever feel happy again." I promise you, you can and will *if* you allow yourself to. I said the same thing. You hear many people say, "I don't have a choice." Everyone has a choice. Someone out there needs you to keep living. Choose to live.

Please don't suppress your grief. It's essential to allow yourself to feel what you feel and work through it, or it will surface years later. Men and women tend to grieve differently. Many men are quiet, causing others to think they have moved on already. That is not the case as most men hold in their grief. Children may feel they are to blame, so be gentle. Ask them if they feel like talking. My daughter Nicole has hardly ever shown any emotion about Mike since his death. Five years after his death, I asked her why she doesn't. She said that his death was so traumatic that she tries not to think about it. She said she never wants to feel that way ever again. I have noticed she's more closed off and keeps her distance, not getting too close to people emotionally.

A central task is for you to try and maintain some safety and order by surrounding yourself with positive people. People that ask you about your loved one who calls or meet you for a meal or coffee. Taking care of yourself is imperative, whether it's through yoga, exercise, meditation, travel, or reading. While sleep can be elusive, it is essential. A healthy diet is also vital. Bad food can make you feel sluggish and depressed. I suggest reading the book *Genius Foods,* by Max Lugavere. You don't have to get carried away. Don't feel you can't have fries once in a while. Think of your body as a car. If you owned a Rolls-Royce, would you put bad oil in it? Of course not; then why put bad food into your body? Do you know why Rolls-Royce doesn't have commercials? Because they know their worth. Do you know your worth? Do you value yourself?

What you eat now determines what your old age could be like for you. By the time something wrong happens, it's usually too late to do anything about it. I'm sure you know many people who've experienced that. We've all heard the saying, "You are what you eat." I am also a realist who knows this is the best we are going to feel right now, (If you're 50 and above). Don't take that to mean you can't make improvements to your health and well-being. I'm experiencing more aches and pains, yet I take care of myself pretty well. Try to walk at least twenty minutes, three times a week if you can; it's an antidepressant. Stay away from alcohol which is a depressant. A glass of wine now and again is relaxing. Did you know that a twenty-second hug produces oxytocin, which is nature's antidepressant and anti-anxiety hormone? Give a hug. Get a hug.

In time, you will come to see positive changes in yourself and how you look at life, by not sweating the small stuff. I pick my battles because if I can survive my son's suicide, I can survive just about anything. Certain things don't bother me like they used to. Your priorities will change—maybe you can donate your time to a charity or at a nursing home once in a while. Many nursing home residents don't have any family to visit them and would love a visitor. Helping others when you're down will help you as well. It can keep you from thinking of your problems when you're helping others. I've noticed I have become more compassionate and understanding, realizing that other people have struggles in their life, too. I give people more of my time, even when I don't have time to give. I stand in line at the grocery store and think to myself; *I wonder what sorrows this person has? What sadness is behind that smile?* I try to be more patient, to treat a server with service that is not up to par, kinder. We don't know whether that person's spouse has just left them alone with four children.

"Unexpected kindness is the most powerful, least costly, and most underrated agent of human change."
Bob Kerrey

Final Thoughts I'd Like to Leave You With

Mental illness can and sometimes does lead to suicide. One in four people will have a mental illness. We all live in a busy world, and some are unaware of the troubles of other's lives. Can't we remember that as a member of the human race, helping those in need may indeed be lifesaving? Inform yourself of the signs of mental illness. Just because some people may be irrational or withdrawn does not mean they are crazy; they have a disease just like any other disease. Why do I say this? Because I've heard many people say, "I don't want to get involved," or "He/she is a pain in the ass." Can't we try to remember they are sick and need help? Are we all *that* busy? How do *you* get involved in the life of a friend or family member who has a problem? How do *they* show up in yours when you need one?

Enough hate and unkindness already exist in our country. I'm asking you to take a *moment* to ask those that might be in need, "Are you ok?" "How can I help you?" A phone call to a hotline may be all they need. What if that friend or loved one took their life, and you never had the time for them? How would you feel then? Many don't see the signs or even know what the symptoms are. That's why I'm asking you to open your eyes. Look at what is going on around the world today. It's the *actions* that *lead up* to suicide that go *unnoticed*.

Some people feel they'll need to *fix* that person or *cure* them. No, all that's required is just a little of your time—a phone call or stopping by to check on them. I have been saying for some time that our country has become *"Me* the People of the United States." I have heard many say, "Let them take care of themselves; I have my issues."

To be truthful, most don't care—they just don't. Isn't their life just as important as yours? Wouldn't you want someone to help you if you needed it? Has human suffering and life become that unimportant?

We live in such a busy world: people in a hurry, self-absorbed, instant gratification, addicted to gadgets, more broken homes with one parent, more addiction to certain drugs, bullying, massive narcissism, addiction to reality shows, and on and on. Yes, I'm concerned over what I see.

Don't get me wrong—many good people still exist. I just feel that society has become so independent. Consider that maybe someone else *isn't* like you and may need or want your help. Again, for children and adults between the ages of 15-24, suicide is the second leading cause of death! How can *we* change this? Change won't happen if *we* don't change.

What will it take for people to care? Losing one of their own? Suicide is up by 40%.

Clinical depression isn't something you choose. Not only is it hard on the person who suffers, but also on the people who care about them. Many that suffer are afraid that their illness may affect their job, partner, or finances and cause the loss of their home, their job, friends, and family. Life can start to unravel, causing them to spiral. What are they going to do with all the guilt, anger, pain, and feelings of being overwhelmed?

I repeat, **untreated depression is the number one cause of suicide** (Suicide.org). Most people that suffer will not come forward to ask for help as they feel they are a burden or a problem for those that love them. Many families will tell the person that suffers to get over it. The sufferer feels alone. People don't realize the seriousness of the condition until it's too late. It is a disease just like any other disease! You wouldn't tell someone, "It's just cancer; get over it." I've heard many people ask, "What do *you* have to be depressed about?" Please don't say that. You have no idea what is going on inside a person, no matter how good they look on the outside.

Knowing the signs of depression would be an excellent place to start, as many may not connect them to depression. I have listed the signs in Chapter Four. Please reach out to someone you know who can use your help. Please wake up and take a closer look at those around you.

You can make a difference. Please be a part of helping to save a life.

In this book, I have shared with you my journey and observations I have learned along the way to help guide you in dealing with grief from the loss of a loved one from suicide. This book can also help guide you in dealing with the underlying causes of depression and understanding how it can affect your life. Suggestions that may help you if you suffer from depression, PTSD or both have been included in my book. Everything I have shared is my journey and not to be prescriptive, but to provide suggestions. I hope that it may be able to save you heartache and time searching.

Grief can affect you in several different ways and cause feelings or things to happen that you won't expect. There is no right or wrong. Be prepared for what people will say and just know they mean well. Go easy on yourself.

Shock is your body's way of protecting you. Denial may also be present. The fog usually lifts by the second year, and then reality hits you. If not very careful, depression can make it easy to escape through alcohol, food binging, under-eating, gambling, drugs, and overspending. No one wants to believe such devastation and loss has occurred. Allow yourself the time you need to heal. Don't allow others to be hard on you.

The seven stages of grief include shock, denial, anger, bargaining, depression, testing, and acceptance. Review the second chapter for details about each step.

For those with depression or PTSD or both, triggers can zap the life out of you and can make you care about nothing. It can take you to hell—I know, I lived there. When I started to spiral, my mind kept going over and over all that I'd just lost. Comparing your life to others' experiences can also be disastrous for you. *DO NOT ALLOW YOURSELF TO DO THIS*. Remember, suicide is never the answer! Please, do not remain in denial about this. Losing hope can be very dangerous. If you are feeling that way, do not wait to seek help. Please refer to Chapter Four to understand the difference between **active** suicidal ideation and **passive** suicidal ideation.

If you've experienced multiple losses as I did, reach out to support groups or your religious affiliation to connect with people who share a similar loss. Individual books may be helpful. Seek the company of those whom you feel good with, who feed your soul. If you suffer from depression that you can't shake or have suicidal thoughts, please seek help immediately. Call the Lifeline: 1-800-273-8255 (USA only).

I created AftermathofSuicide.com to help people receive support, advice, and to take advantage of the services I offer. Services from someone who not only lived through the loss of a child to suicide and survived but has a mental illness and PTSD. I understand the hell you may be living in. I received more help from strangers than from friends or family. Recognize that many people may leave your life; those who do are not your real friends. Let them go and focus on *you*. Surround yourself with people who make you feel loved.

I met an older woman named Nora at a support group in Carlsbad, California, in 2015, who befriended me. What a beautiful outlook on life she has. You can meet some great people in support groups. Out of my tragedy, I have received gifts I did not have. Despite our age difference at eight-eight, she still travels and drives! We even speak often. What an inspiration she is.

I think the fourth chapter is the most important in this book. It's not solely for suicide loss survivors. The information provided can help those who battle depression or PTSD or both. Asking for help is brave, so do not feel embarrassed. You are not a burden. Only *YOU* can take the first step to get help. If you're depressed for longer than a month, please *seek out a clinician who understands suicide loss or mental illness.* Finding the right one is so crucial because getting misdiagnosed can prolong the time it takes to recover. Seeking out the *right clinician* can be the difference between life or death. Please be proactive. Talk to them about medication if you're open to it. Most people are not going to take your hand and lead you. No one did that for me. ***Your life is worth it.*** As Dr. Phil has said, "You cannot change what you do not acknowledge."

When you're not receiving the right care, falling into a deep depression can be very dangerous. Please start the grief work that I discussed in Chapter Two as soon as you can. Although my son has been dead five years, I still am not through all seven stages of grief yet and truthfully may never be. They do not have a set time frame. Keep in mind that men and women grieve differently. While many men who are grieving may be quiet about it, this does not mean they have moved on already or aren't grieving. Most men hold it in, feeling the need to keep everything together. Children also grieve differently and may think as if they are to blame somehow. Be gentle and ask them if they feel like talking. Please do not take them to a therapist against their will or force them to talk.

If you suffer from depression, people may ask you, "What do you have to be depressed about?" How do you begin to answer that? They will never understand the answer. Me, I walk away. You can't explain depression to people who don't suffer from it. People don't realize depression is killing us. Please, don't ever say that to someone unless you know them well or are joking around. Remember, sadness and depression are not the same. The symptoms of depression are quite extensive and vary from person to person. One out of every six youths between the age of 15-24 in the US experience some form of a mental health disorder each year. Many of the symptoms are not commonly associated with depression by most people. Remember, many do not think children can be depressed.

Read the myths and facts about suicide again. If you are in crisis or you know someone who may be, please call the crisis line at 1-800-273-8255.

Learning and sharing statistics related to suicide and depression can help to diminish the stigma associated with mental illness.

Symptoms of PTSD often are brought on by triggers specific to your trauma or experience. Once you become aware of them, do your best to avoid them. PTSD can also bring on panic/anxiety attacks without warning. Remember to take slow breaths in your nose and out your mouth.

By sharing some insight into my son, Mike, I showed that he was more than just a depressed man who suffered from his demons. He was also not proactive in helping himself, and look where it got him? I also felt it was essential to identify some of the signs of depression for those who have small children and may know very little about mental illness and its symptoms. Mike's suicide was only a part of him among all the other moments of laughter, fun, love for his family, gifted intelligence, and so much more.

Grief can bring you to your knees anytime, anywhere. Do not apologize if this happens or be ashamed of sharing your story; it can inspire others. Remember J.K. Rowling's story. When you can begin to switch from grief to memories of the happy times and laughter, you'll know you are healing and progressing. Please don't pressure yourself to please others. If you have been taking care of yourself and seeking needed help, you will start to notice your desire to do things even though previously, you'd felt like never leaving the house.

If you struggle with mental illness or PTSD and feel like you're ready to get out, speak with your friends and family. You deserve to be happy. I suggest that you continue with therapy, which can be very helpful. I still attend my therapy every two weeks. I even receive therapy through Skype or by phone when I'm unable to be there in person. DO NOT make your recovery your last priority. Your life is worth it. No excuses. If you're not well, how can you be the parent your children need? The wife or husband your spouse needs? A good sibling? There will be days when you find yourself taking two steps forward and three steps back. It's ok, don't beat yourself up. Not wanting to let go of your loved one is perfectly normal. Listen to your instincts; do what's best for *you,* even if it's staying in bed all day.

Get plenty of sleep, some form of exercise a few days a week, and eat a healthy diet. In time, you will observe positive changes in your outlook and habits. Giving more of your time to help others can help you forget your problems. Try to limit your stressors. Remember, handle one thing at a time.

If you would like to ask me a personal question about my journey, you can reach out to me on my website on the "Contact Jill" page.

The wave in my logo at AftermathofSuicide.com represents the tsunami that hit me when I received the news that my son was found dead. The sun that shines through the waves represents the light that is visible in the distance. We are *survivors—you* **are a** *survivor.*

To anyone who has had suicidal thoughts this past year—I'm glad you're still here.

Please visit my website to learn more about
me and the services I offer.

Call Lifeline: 1-800-273-8255 (USA only)

Text: HOME to 741741 (Crisis Text Line - USA only)

1-800-959-8277 (USA only)

https://suicidepreventionlifeline.org

https://suicidepreventionlifeline.org/help-yourself/veterans/

Write to me at jill@aftermathofsuicide.com

References

Fuller, K. "Mental Health Conditions Seen in Childhood." October 2019. National Alliance on Mental Health.

Gutin, Nina J. "Helping survivors in the aftermath of suicide loss." *Current Psychiatry*, August 2018. MDedge.

Lugavere, Max. *Genius Foods*, 2018.

Mayo Clinic, https://www.mayoclinic.org/

Suicide Awareness Voices of Education, https://save.org/

Suicide.org, http://suicide.org

US Department of Veterans Affairs, https://www.mentalhealth.va.gov/

Verywell Mind, https://www.verywellmind.com/

World Health Organization, https://www.who.int/

Lightning Source UK Ltd.
Milton Keynes UK
UKHW020644060720
366003UK00006B/144